Weapons of War

The War on Terrorism

By John Hamilton

Visit us at
www.abdopub.com

Published by ABDO & Daughters, an imprint of ABDO Publishing Company, 4940 Viking Drive, Suite 622, Edina, Minnesota 55435. Copyright ©2002 by Abdo Consulting Group, Inc. International copyrights reserved in all countries. No part of this book may be reproduced in any form without written permission from the publisher.

Printed in the United States.

Edited by Paul Joseph
Graphic Design: John Hamilton
Cover Design: Mighty Media
Illustrations: John Hamilton
Photos: DoD

Library of Congress Cataloging-in-Publication Data

Hamilton, John , 1959-
    Weapons of war / John Hamilton.
      p. cm. — (War on terrorism)
    Includes index.
    Summary: Briefly describes the history and gives examples of military
    weapons and technology including various types of ships, guns, missiles,
    planes, tanks, and weapons of mass destruction.
    ISBN 1-57765-673-3
     1. Military weapons—Juvenile literature. [1. Military weapons.]   I.
    Title. II. Series.
     U815 .H29 2002
     623.4—dc21
                                                          2001055991

Table of Contents

Vertical Flight

A pair of U.S. Air Force F-16 Fighting Falcons climb skyward while on a mission near Great Falls, Montana.

Fighters and Close Air Support

A NATION WITH A GREAT AIR FORCE HAS A huge advantage because it gains control of the skies early in a war. Fighter planes have several missions. Reconnaissance missions tell commanders where the enemy is, how big its forces are, if they're moving, and where. Interception missions involve combat fighters battling each other in the air.

In the war in Afghanistan, enemy planes were destroyed before they could even get in the air. This was done with strike missions, which attack enemy planes, airports, radar sites, tanks, or other targets. Ground commanders can call in fighters and close air support aircraft on short notice. Fighters can attack targets both on the ground and in the air.

F-14 Tomcat
Primary function: Carrier-based multirole strike fighter
Length: 62 feet (19 m)
Wingspan: 64 feet (20 m)
Speed: 1,551 mph (2,496 km/h)
Armament: One M61A1/A2 Vulcan 20mm cannon
Crew: Pilot and radar intercept officer

Featured in the Tom Cruise movie *Top Gun*, the U.S. Navy's F-14 Tomcat is a fast and nimble fighter. Its main job is to protect ships from enemy planes. Launched from aircraft carriers, the Tomcat is a supersonic, twin-engine jet. It carries advanced electronics that track many targets at the same time. The F-14's wings can sweep forward, which gives it the lift needed for slow flying. When the wings are swept back, the dart-like Tomcat cuts through the air at two times the speed of sound.

In addition to air-to-air combat, the F-14 can also strike targets on the ground. Launched from aircraft carriers in the Arabian Sea and the Persian Gulf, Tomcats fired smart bombs at targets in Afghanistan. Other aircraft painted the targets with lasers to help the bombs find their way with greater accuracy.

F/A-18 Hornet
Primary function: Multirole attack and fighter aircraft
Speed: 1,320 mph (2,124 km/h)
Length: 56 feet (17 m)
Wingspan: 38 feet (12 m)
Armament: One M61A1/A2 Vulcan 20mm cannon
Crew: Pilot only

The U.S. Navy and Marine Corps' F/A-18 Hornet is a single-seated jet fighter that can operate from either aircraft carriers or land bases. The F/A-18 is a strike fighter, which means it was designed to attack targets both in the air and on the ground, such as missile sites or command bunkers.

The Hornet uses advanced electronics to track targets. It also is a nimble fighter, which helps pilots dodge enemy fighters or missiles. The F/A-18 is reliable and easy to maintain. Its one shortcoming is its limited range of flight compared with other fighters, but this is made up for on long missions with midair refueling by tanker planes.

F-117A Nighthawk
Primary function: Attack fighter
Speed: 645 mph (1,038 km/h)
Length: 66 feet (20 m)
Wingspan: 43 feet (13 m)
Crew: Pilot only

The U.S. Air Force **F-117A Nighthawk** is the first plane to use stealth technology. It has a very small footprint on enemy radar screens, thanks to its shape and special black paint. Because it is so hard to detect, it often flies into highly defended enemy territory to destroy air defenses and radar sites. This allows other waves of U.S. planes to complete their jobs. The F-117A depends on low flying and its stealthy design for its defense. In many cases, enemies don't know a Nighthawk is attacking until they hear bomb explosions. By then, the F-117A has left the scene.

Nighthawks normally deliver two Paveway 2,000-pound (907-kg) laser-guided bombs. They can also carry AGM-65 Maverick air-to-surface missiles, or AGM-88 antiradar missiles.

F-15E Strike Eagle
Primary function: Air-to-ground attack
Speed: 1,875 mph (3,017 km/h)
Length: 64 feet (20 m)
Wingspan: 43 feet (13 m)
Armament: Air-to-air and air-to-ground missiles
Crew: One or two

The U.S. Air Force F15-E Strike Eagle is a dual-purpose jet fighter. It can attack targets in the air and on the ground. Its main purpose is to strike ground targets. The F15-E has a sophisticated system of electronics that helps it fly low, day or night, even in bad weather. Since it's a dual-role fighter, it can fight its way to a target from far away, destroy the enemy, and then fight its way back to home base.

The rear cockpit of the F15-E holds the weapons systems officer. While the pilot flies the plane, the weapons officer watches computer screens to track and fire on several targets at once.

F-16 Fighting Falcon
Primary function: Multirole fighter jet
Speed: 1,500 mph (2,414 km/h)
Length: 49 feet (15 m)
Wingspan: 33 feet (10 m)
Armament: Air-to-air combat and
air-to-surface attack munitions
Crew: One or two

The **F-16 Fighting Falcon** is the U.S. Air Force's highly maneuverable, lightweight fighter aircraft. It was designed to fight during the day, but modern electronics have made it a fearsome weapon even at night, and in bad weather.

The F-16 is a dual-purpose fighter, made to fight enemy aircraft and bomb targets on the ground. It's a high-performance aircraft that can make sharp turns at high speed, which helps it evade enemy planes or missiles. Many pilots consider the F-16 to be the most agile fighter jet in the world.

Advanced electronics help the F-16 accurately bomb targets on the ground, and its great agility means it can fight its way out of almost any air-to-air combat situation.

AC-130H/U Gunship
Primary function: Close air support
Speed: 300 mph (483 km/h)
Length: 98 feet (30 m)
Wingspan: 133 feet (41 m)
Armament: AC-130H/U: 40mm cannon and 105mm cannon; AC-130U: 25mm gun
Crew: Five officers (pilot, co-pilot, navigator, fire control officer, electronic warfare officer) and eight enlisted (flight engineer, TV operator, infrared detection set operator, loadmaster, four aerial gunners)

The AC-130 "Spectre" Gunship is a heavy-hitting armed aircraft. Its main mission is to protect soldiers on the ground. It is especially valuable at night in assisting special operations troops, such as Army Rangers or Delta Force commandos.

To attack units on the ground, the AC-130 slowly circles an area and tilts downward so that gunners can fire out the side of the aircraft. The Spectre has several different kinds of weapons. These include a 25mm Gatling gun, a 40mm Bofors cannon, and a 105mm cannon.

With weapons like these, the AC-130 can destroy anything from enemy troops to tanks. It can also track and shoot at separate targets up to one mile (1.6 km) apart.

B-52 Takeoff

A B-52 Stratofortress long-range bomber takes off from an airfield, with another B-52 following close behind.

Long-Range Bombers

BOMBERS ARE USUALLY MUCH BIGGER THAN fighter aircraft. They are designed this way so that they can deliver many bombs at once to targets on the ground. As of November 2001, Air Force B-2, B-1, and B-52 bombers used more than 80 percent of the tonnage dropped on combat missions over Afghanistan. In a month's time, Air Force bombers flew more than 600 times, including strike missions against al-Qaeda and Taliban targets in Afghanistan. These targets included early-warning radars, ground forces, command and control facilities, al-Qaeda buildings, airfields, and aircraft.

Bombers aren't as fast or maneuverable as fighters. Because of this, they are more vulnerable to enemy planes or missiles. For protection, bombers often have fighter escorts to ward off the enemy. Some bombers, such as the B-2 Spirit, protect themselves by being stealthy.

B1-B Lancer
Primary function: Long-range heavy bomber
Length: 146 feet (45 m)
Wingspan: 137 feet (42 m)
Speed: 900+ mph (1,448+ km/h)
Range: 6,400 miles (10,298 km)
Armament: Short-range attack missiles, bombs, and cruise missiles
Crew: Four (aircraft commander, co-pilot, offensive systems officer, defensive systems officer)

The United States developed the **B1-B Lancer** during the Cold War in order to drop nuclear bombs on the former Soviet Union. Today, it is the only bomber in the U.S. fleet that flies faster than sound. Not only is it fast, the Lancer also flies at low altitudes, even in bad weather, thanks to special electronics with built-in maps of the enemy terrain.

Since the Soviet Union no longer exists, the threat of global nuclear war has lessened. The B1-B bomber can now carry conventional bombs. It holds up to 84 conventional 500-pound (227-kg) bombs, 30 cluster bombs, or 24 "smart bombs" that weigh 2,000 pounds (907 kg) each. Smart bombs use special electronics that guide them to within 40 feet (12 m) of their targets.

The B1-B Lancer has a flight range of about 6,400 miles (10,300 km). During the war in Afghanistan, most B1-B Lancer bombers were launched from the Diego Garcia Air Base, an island in the middle of the Indian Ocean, south of Afghanistan.

B-52 Stratofortress
Primary function: Heavy bomber
Speed: 650 mph (1,046 km/h)
Range: 8,800 miles (14,159 km)
Length: 159 feet (48 m)
Wingspan: 185 feet (56 m)
Armament: 70,000 pounds (31,751 kg) of mixed weapons: bombs, mines, and missiles
Crew: Five (aircraft commander, pilot, radar navigator, navigator, electronic warfare officer)

The **B-52 Stratofortress** long-range bomber has been the workhorse of the U.S. Air Force since it started flying in the 1950s. It saw heavy use dropping bombs during the Vietnam War. Today, even though it keeps its original design and main structure, the B-52 has been completely refitted with modern engines, flight control electronics, and electronic defense equipment.

The B-52 can carry both conventional and nuclear bombs. It can also launch cruise missiles. It has one of the largest payload capacities of any U.S. bomber. Because it can carry such heavy loads, it is often used in carpet-bombing missions. Carpet-bombing uses conventional bombs. Enemy territory is hit with many bombs at once. Carpet-bombing doesn't always destroy a target, but it is very effective in terrifying the enemy.

During the war in Afghanistan most B-52s were launched from the Diego Garcia Air Base, an island in the middle of the Indian Ocean, south of Afghanistan.

B-2 Spirit
Primary function: Multirole heavy bomber
Length: 69 feet (21 m)
Wingspan: 172 feet (52 m)
Speed: High subsonic
Range: 6,900 miles (11,102 km)
Armament: Conventional or nuclear weapons
Crew: Two pilots

Many bombing missions today call for planes to fly long distances deep into enemy territory, with no help from friendly fighter jets. If a bomber is detected, enemy fighters try to intercept and shoot it down. Or, missiles streak up from the ground to destroy the bomber. In order for a bomber crew to carry out a mission and come back alive, the element of surprise is very important.

The **B-2 Spirit** "stealth" bomber has a wingspan about half the length of a football field, but on a radar screen it looks as small as a bird. The B-2 was designed to have all its surfaces curved, with no sharp angles to cause blips on radar. Every edge and screw is covered with special tape and paint that scatters radar signals. And instead of constructing the plane with aluminum, like most planes, the Air Force made the B-2 from graphite. Any noisy signals from electronic equipment inside the plane are trapped and absorbed.

To hide from heat-seeking missiles, the B-2 has engines stored deep within the plane. Hot exhaust gasses are cooled before they leave the B-2 through special vents on top of the wings. By venting this way, enemy planes flying lower than the B-2 have a hard time finding the bomber with heat-seeking electronic equipment. Even if the B-2 is detected, it flies high, up to 50,000 feet (15,240 m), which puts it out of range of most ground-based anti-aircraft missiles.

The B-2 cuts through the air easily, and it's lighter than other bombers because of its graphite construction. By adding quiet, efficient engines, the Air Force created a bomber that flies much quieter than other planes. The B-2 is painted black, making it even harder to detect, especially at night.

Because of their stealth abilities, B-2 Spirit bombers are used in the first hours of an attack to destroy the enemy's command centers and anti-aircraft weapons.

The B-2 can carry many kinds of bombs, nuclear and conventional. In the first months of the war in Afghanistan they dropped free-falling bombs that were fitted with global positioning devices, which make the bombs more accurate. The Air Force calls these kinds of bombs Joint Direct Attack Munitions (JDAM).

B-2's are easily damaged in severe weather by hail, freezing rain, and moisture. They are costly to repair, so the fleet of B-2's is housed in the United States in special hangers. Even so, they can still strike targets all over the world, with a flight range of about 6,900 miles (11,104 km) (around the world with one midflight refueling). B-2 bombers used in the war in Afghanistan started their missions from Whiteman Air Force Base in Missouri.

The B-2 Spirit bomber is an amazing machine, but high technology comes with a high price. Each of the 21 bombers in the fleet cost American taxpayers $2.1 billion.

B-2 Attack

On a practice mission over Alaska, a B-2 drops a nuclear-tipped "bunker buster" bomb. (The weapon carried a dummy warhead.)

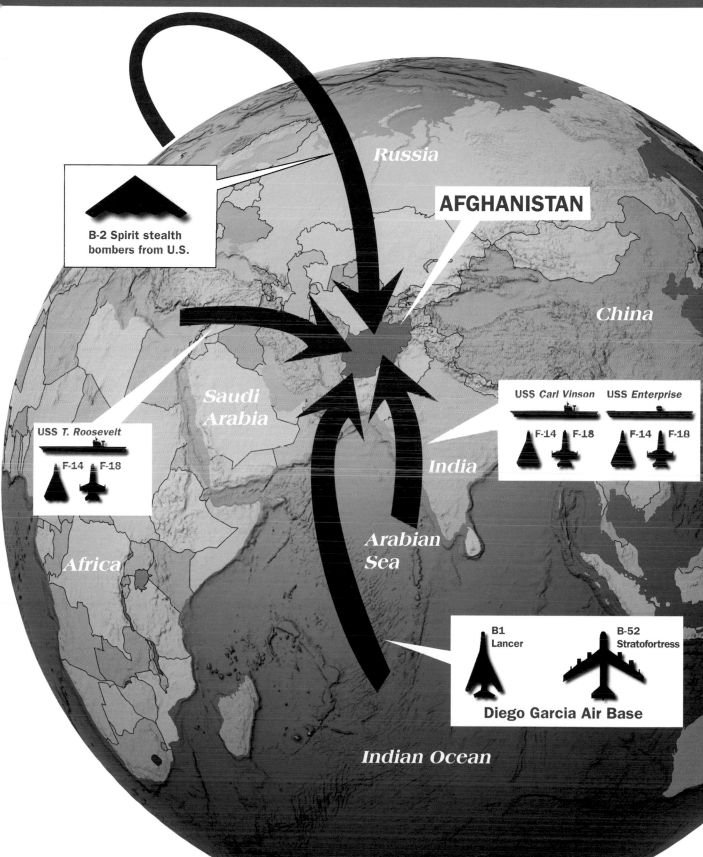

B-2 Spirit stealth bombers from U.S.

AFGHANISTAN

Russia

China

Saudi Arabia

USS *Carl Vinson*   USS *Enterprise*

F-14   F-18   F-14   F-18

India

USS *T. Roosevelt*

F-14   F-18

Africa

Arabian Sea

B1 Lancer   B-52 Stratofortress

Diego Garcia Air Base

Indian Ocean

Pave Low In Action

A U.S. Air Force Pave Low heavy-lift, long-range helicopter.

Helicopters

A S THE WAR IN AFGHANISTAN SHIFTS TO A war on the ground, helicopters will become an important part of the United States' arsenal. Helicopters can quickly move troops in and out of enemy territory. Some helicopters are designed to attack the enemy, especially tanks and other armored targets. With today's advanced electronics, helicopters are deadly weapons that can fly day or night, no matter the weather conditions.

The MH-53J Pave Low (pictured at left) is the largest and most powerful helicopter used by the U.S. Air Force. The Pave Low's mission is to fly, from far away, into enemy territory without being detected. Special forces teams often use the Pave Low at night, even in bad weather, to sneak in close to the enemy. The Pave Low can lift heavy loads, which makes it good for resupplying special operations troops. It can carry 37 passengers or 13,000 pounds (5,897 kg) of cargo.

The Pave Low has infrared sensors and terrain-avoidance radar. This technology helps it fly at night, and also allows it to fly close to the ground. Projected map displays and Global Positioning Systems (GPS) also help the pilots avoid obstacles.

MH-53J Pave Low (pictured at left)
Primary function: Heavy-lift, long-range penetration
Speed: 165 mph (265 km/h)
Armament: Up to three 7.62 mm miniguns or .50-caliber machine guns
Crew: Two pilots, two flight engineers, and two aerial gunners

AH-64D Apache Helicopter
Primary function: Multimission attack helicopter
Speed: 189 mph (304 km/h)
Armament: Hellfire anti-tank missiles, rockets, 30mm cannon
Crew: Two

The **AH-64D Apache** is the U.S. Army's main gunship and anti-tank helicopter. Even though it can detect and track any moving vehicle under almost any conditions, the Apache is used mainly as a tank destroyer. It is armed with 16 laser-guided Hellfire missiles or 76 70mm rockets. It also has an automatic cannon that can shoot up to 1,200 rounds of high-explosive bullets.

The Apache is fast, maneuverable, and hard to see on radar screens. It leads the way in surprise attacks, clearing enemy areas of tanks and early-warning radar so that friendly ground forces can start their assault. In Desert Storm in 1991, a group of Apaches destroyed 50 Iraqi tanks in a single battle.

UH-60 Blackhawk Helicopter
Primary function: Air assault and general support missions
Speed: 184 mph (296 km/h)
Armament: Two 7.62mm miniguns
Crew: Two pilots, one crew chief, one door gunner

The **UH-60 Blackhawk** is a heavy-lift helicopter designed to bring troops and equipment far into enemy territory. It is the U.S. Army's chief tactical transport. It can be used for moving wounded soldiers off the battlefield, search and rescue, night operations, electronic warfare, and reconnaissance.

There are two other versions of the UH-60 Blackhawk that are used by special forces teams. The MH-60K and MH-60G are special Blackhawks designed with enhanced electronics that help with navigation and self-defense. The electronic improvements include radar-warning sensors and electronic jammers. Flare dispensers fool missiles fired at the Blackhawk.

MH-47E Chinook Helicopter

Primary function: Transport, medical evacuation, search and recovery
Speed:183 mph (295 km/h)
Armament: 7.62mm minigun, M-60D 7.62mm machine gun
Crew: Two pilots

The **MH-47E Chinook** is a transport helicopter, the largest in service with U.S. and British armies. It has highly advanced flight electronics and can fly long distances, day or night, under many weather conditions. Special operations teams sometimes use the Chinook on secret, deep-penetration missions. Its electronics let the pilot fly low to the ground, evading enemy radar.

OH 58D Kiowa Helicopter
Primary function: Scouting missions
Speed: 139 mph (224 km/h)
Armament: Hellfire and Stinger missiles, rockets, .50-caliber machine gun
Crew: Two pilots

The **Kiowa** is used by both the U.S. Army and Navy, mainly as a scout aircraft. The Kiowa finds and observes the enemy, and then directs fire to the target, either by attack aircraft or ground forces. Some Kiowa helicopters are fitted with Hellfire missiles, which are used mainly to destroy tanks. Some also carry Stinger air-to-air missiles for protection against enemy helicopters.

Midair Refueling

A U.S. Air Force KC-135 refuels an F-111 bomber.

WISCON

KC-135 Stratotanker
Primary function: Aerial refueling and airlift
Speed: 530 mph (853 km/h)
Length: 136 feet (41 m)
Wingspan: 131 feet (40 m)
Crew: Four (pilot, co-pilot, navigator, boom operator)

Support Aircraft

E ven though they don't usually take part in combat, there are many aircraft that are very important for winning a war. Their missions include transporting supplies and fuel, coordinating friendly aircraft and ground fire, and finding the enemy.

Modeled after the Boeing 707 commercial jetliner, the U.S. Air Force's **KC-135 Stratotanker's** main mission is to refuel fighters and bombers in midair. It uses a flying boom that trails the KC-135 and hooks up to other planes equipped with a special probe. Once the boom is attached, fuel is pumped through it. An operator at the rear of the plane controls the boom. Midair refueling means that combat aircraft are no longer limited by fuel supplies, and can spend more time in the air completing their missions.

Depending on how the fuel storage is arranged, KC-135s can carry about 83,000 pounds (37,648 kg) of cargo. In addition to carrying fuel, the Stratotanker has a cargo deck above the refueling system that can hold about 130 troops.

C-17 Globemaster
Primary Function: Cargo and troop transport
Max payload: 170,900 pounds (77,519 kg)
Speed: Up to 518 mph (834 km/h)
Length: 175 feet (53 m)
Wingspan: 170 feet (52 m)
Crew: Three (two pilots and one loadmaster)

The newest of the U.S. military's transport craft, the **C-17 Globemaster**, entered service in 1993. It is a long-range, heavy-lift cargo plane. It can lift wide and heavy items, such as tanks. It can land at airfields usually open only to much smaller transport aircraft. The Globemaster can carry one M1 Abrams tank or three Bradley armored fighting vehicles. Or it can carry up to three Apache helicopters. Up to 102 paratroopers can also be carried and dropped over the battlefield.

The **Joint Surveillance Target Attack Radar System** (**Joint STARS**) (pictured at right) is an advanced targeting and battle management system. Joint STARS (also called JSTARS) aircraft are modified Boeing 707 jetliners that act as airborne battle managers. They can track enemy troops and vehicles, then relay that information to commanders on the ground. Ground commanders can then get a better idea of the enemy situation and decide how best to attack or defend.

RQ-1 Predator
Primary function: Surveillance and target acquisition
Speed: Up to 140 mph (225 km/h)
Range: 454 miles (730 km)
Length: 27 feet (8 m)
Wingspan: 49 feet (15 m)

The **Predator** (pictured above) is a drone that flies slowly over enemy territory, sending back images that tell military planners about terrain, people, and buildings. It can stay in the air for 24 hours. In Afghanistan, Predator drones revealed details of terrorist camps without endangering any pilots. Operators on the ground used infrared cameras on the Predator to view people, vehicles, and buildings up to 20 miles (32 km) away.

Some Predators have Hellfire missiles mounted under their wings. Operators on the ground can fire these at armored vehicles, like tanks.

E-8C Joint STARS
Primary function: Airborne battle management
Speed (Cruising): 523 mph (842 km/h)
Crew: Four (flight crew, plus mission crew of 15)

Air Strike

An Air Force strike fighter drops a payload of bombs over its target.

Bombs and Missiles

ACRUISE MISSILE IS A GUIDED WEAPON THAT flies like a small airplane very close to the ground. Tomahawk cruise missiles are naval weapons launched from ships or submarines. The AGM-86B/C is a bigger version air-launched from B-52 or B-1 bombers.

Cruise missiles can be launched from many hundreds of miles away, yet are very accurate. With a range of about 1,000 miles (1,609 km), it's like launching from New York City and hitting a target no bigger than a garage door in Minnesota.

Tomahawk Cruise Missile
Range: 1,000 miles (1,609 km)
Length: 14 to 20 feet (4.2 to 6 m)
Wingspan: 8.5 feet (2.4 m)
Guidance: Uses Global Positioning System (GPS) to reach targets
Launch: Launches from ships or submarine torpedo tubes

Because cruise missiles fly so low to the ground, closely hugging every hill and valley, they are very difficult to spot on radar. This is called "flying under the radar." They are also fast, flying at 550 miles per hour (885 km/h), making them even more difficult to shoot down.

When a cruise missile strikes its target, it detonates a 1,000-pound (454-kg) bomb. The cruise missile itself is destroyed, and hopefully so is the target. Cruise missiles cost between $500,000 and $1 million each, so it's an expensive way to drop a bomb. The cost is often worth it, though, because of the missile's accuracy, plus there is no human pilot to worry about getting shot down.

Older Tomahawk cruise missiles are now being fitted with a satellite-based Global Positioning System, which makes them even more precise. Two recent additions to the U.S. arsenal are the SLAM-ER and AGM-154 JSOW short-range cruise missiles. Both can be air-launched from many kinds of aircraft, especially F/A-18 and F-16 fighter jets.

Missile Away!

A Tomahawk cruise missile is launched from a submerged submarine.

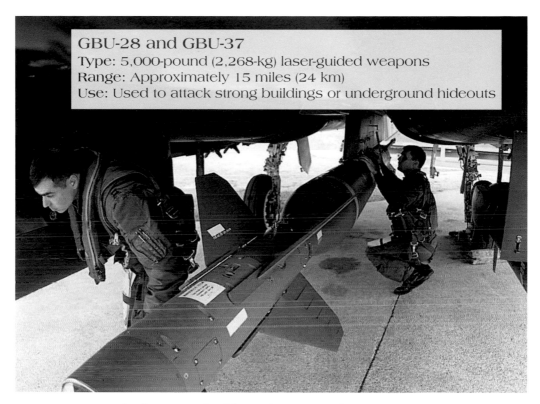

GBU-28 and GBU-37
Type: 5,000-pound (2,268-kg) laser-guided weapons
Range: Approximately 15 miles (24 km)
Use: Used to attack strong buildings or underground hideouts

GBU stands for "guided bomb unit." The GBU-37 is guided to its target by a Global Positioning System (GPS) that uses data from satellites. The GBU-28 is guided when somebody, usually on the ground a safe distance away, shines a laser light on the target. The GBU-28 then follows the spot of energy that is reflected from the target. Wings on the bomb allow it to control spin and make aim adjustments all the way to the target.

The GBU-28 and GBU-37 are sometimes called bunker busters because they are used against targets buried under the earth. Both have 4,400-pound (1,996-kg) warheads that explode after burrowing into the earth, sometimes as deep as 100 feet (30 m) underground, or through 20 feet (6 m) of concrete. The explosions suck most of the air out of the underground tunnel or bunker. Tremendous heat follows, and anything inside is burned or melted.

Cluster Bombs
Type: Air-to-ground bomblets

Cluster bombs contain mini bombs, called bomblets. When dropped from a plane, the cluster bomb opens and spins, releasing the bomblets. Cluster bombs are not meant to be accurate. They work by carpeting large areas of ground. One cluster bomb canister can cover an area the size of four football fields.

When the bomblets explode, either on impact or just above the ground, they release shrapnel in all directions, destroying anything they strike. Cluster bombs are powerful enough to pierce thick metal. They are sometimes used to destroy tanks or other armored vehicles, but are especially devastating to large groups of enemy soldiers.

One problem with cluster bombs is that sometimes they don't explode. Later, innocent civilians can accidentally set them off.

- Global Positioning System (GPS) guidance kit
- Converts existing free-falling bombs into smart weapons

JDAM (pictured above) stands for Joint Direct Attack Munition. It is a low-cost guidance kit attached to a dumb bomb after it is manufactured. With JDAM attached, the bomb becomes a smart weapon, able to use satellite navigation systems to guide it to its target. JDAM weapons are very accurate, and are reliable in any weather. They can be launched from far away and use their navigation system to update the weapon all the way to impact.

The **AGM-154 JSOW** (Joint Standoff Weapon, pictured below) is a highly lethal weapon launched by fighter jets from almost

AGM-154 JSOW
Type: Air-to-ground smart bomb

any altitude. Fired from well outside enemy air defenses, the AGM-154 JSOW is used against many different kinds of targets, from armored vehicles like tanks, to buildings or radar installations. It has a range of about 30 miles (48 km).

Power At Sea

An aircraft carrier battle group shows off its array of surface ships and planes.

Ships

N THE WAR AGAINST TERRORISM IN AFGHANISTAN, IT might seem that the U.S. Navy would have a small role to play since Afghanistan is totally landlocked. The Navy, though, is playing a big part in the war in several ways.

Many Islamic countries neighboring Afghanistan were reluctant to let the U.S. use their air bases. So the U.S. used aircraft carriers to launch fighter jet strikes against terrorist forces. Special forces troops were also housed on Navy ships, ready to move when called to duty. In addition, Navy surface ships, as well as U.S. and United Kingdom submarines, fired cruise missiles. Without the help of the Navy, the fight against terrorism would be much tougher.

Danger Down Below

A frogman swims toward a U.S. Navy nuclear-powered attack submarine.

Floating Airfield

An aircraft carrier cruises on the open sea, its deck filled with planes preparing for action.

Aircraft carriers do not sail alone. They are part of a battle group, which includes a flotilla of support ships. Guided missile destroyers and cruisers help protect the aircraft carriers. Planes constantly buzz around in a protective halo, ready to intercept any enemy aircraft that may attack.

Strike fighter aircraft, including F/A-18 Hornets and F-14 Tomcats, struck Afghanistan after being launched from U.S. aircraft carriers stationed in the Arabian Sea and the Persian Gulf.

The Enterprise Battle Group (as of early November 2001) is stationed near the Arabian Sea. The USS *Enterprise* holds about 6,000 people and 68 aircraft.

The USS *Carl Vinson* is part of a battle group stationed near the Persian Gulf. The USS *Theodore Roosevelt* is in the Mediterranean Sea. These two ships are *Nimitz*-class aircraft carriers, the largest warships ever built. They are 1,089 feet (332 m) long. Fully loaded, they can hold up to 96,700 tons (98,252 metric tons). Each ship can hold up to 85 aircraft.

All three of these aircraft carriers are powered by nuclear reactors. Together with their fleet of support vessels, they can project an awesome amount of power anywhere in the world.

M1A1 Abrams Tank
Length: 26 feet (8 m)
Weight: 126,000 pounds (57,154 kg)
Crew: Four (commander, gunner, loader, driver)

Ground Forces

N THE WAR AGAINST TERRORISM IN AFGHANISTAN, THE U.S. government hopes a collection of rebel Afghan forces called the Northern Alliance will make ground action by the United States unnecessary. If the Northern Alliance fails and the U.S. decides that ground forces are necessary to root out the terrorists, they will have a number of fearsome and battle-tested weapons at their disposal.

The **M1A1 Abrams** (pictured at left) is the U.S. Army and Marine Corps' main battle tank. Many people in the military think the Abrams is the best tank ever built. The M1A1 is huge, weighing 126,000 pounds (57,154 kg). Despite its weight, the Abrams is fast and very mobile. The tank's armor plating is said to be almost impenetrable, and its 120mm smoothbore gun can destroy most enemy tanks at very long range. During Operation Desert Storm in 1991, the Abrams' sighting control system worked well in haze, fog, and swirling sand. Its armor allowed very few penetrating hits, and no crew fatalities.

M2 Bradley Mechanized Infantry Fighting Vehicle
Length: 22 feet (7 m)
Weight: 66,000 pounds (29,937 kg)
Crew: Three (commander, gunner, driver, plus up to six soldiers)

The **M2 Bradley Fighting Vehicle** can carry up to six soldiers along with a crew of three into battle, but it is also good at supporting the M1A1 Abrams main battle tank. The M2 is fast, able to speed into battle at up to 42 miles per hour (68 km/h). It is also highly maneuverable. The M2 is protected by steel armor, and can attack with a 25mm M242 chain gun, twin anti-tank missile launchers, and Stinger surface-to-air missiles.

M109 Paladin
Length: 20 feet (6 m)
Weight: 55,000 pounds (24,948 kg)
Crew: Six (commander, gunner, three ammunition servers, driver)

The **M109 Paladin** 155mm howitzer is a tank-like weapon that can fire many kinds of artillery shells, including high explosives, plus chemical, smoke, and nuclear rounds.

The Paladin is self-propelled, moving around on tracks like a tank. It is also armored like a tank to protect the crew from enemy attack. It fires a 155mm shell to give support for ground troops. It is used, like most artillery, for "indirect fire" support. Troops on the front line, or reconnaissance aircraft, tell the Paladin crew the location of the enemy. The Paladin opens fire on the hostile forces from far away, usually out of sight of where the battle is taking place.

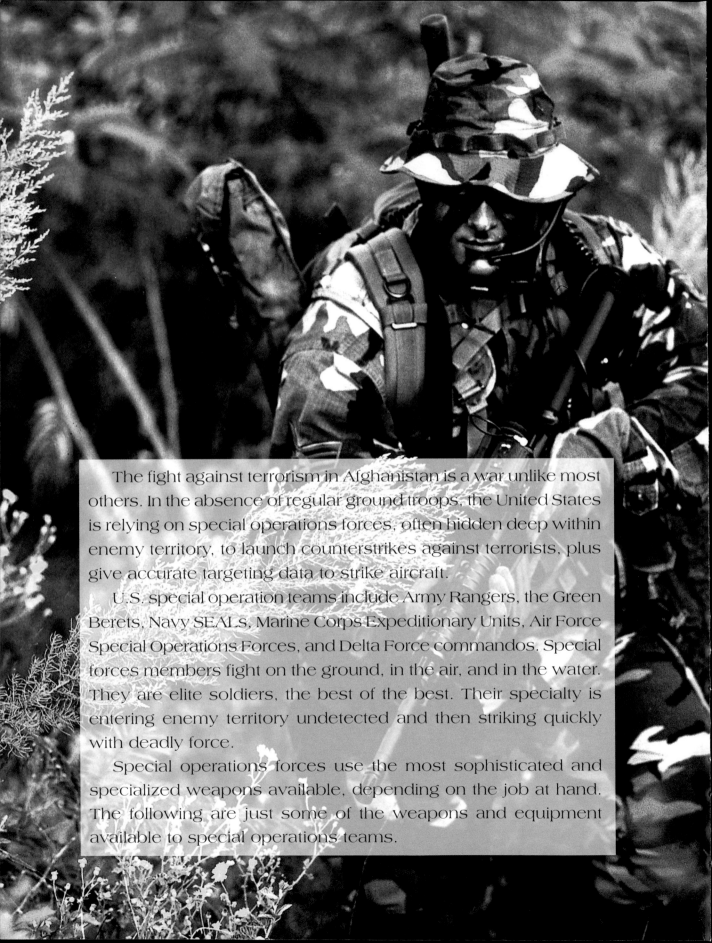

The fight against terrorism in Afghanistan is a war unlike most others. In the absence of regular ground troops, the United States is relying on special operations forces, often hidden deep within enemy territory, to launch counterstrikes against terrorists, plus give accurate targeting data to strike aircraft.

U.S. special operation teams include Army Rangers, the Green Berets, Navy SEALs, Marine Corps Expeditionary Units, Air Force Special Operations Forces, and Delta Force commandos. Special forces members fight on the ground, in the air, and in the water. They are elite soldiers, the best of the best. Their specialty is entering enemy territory undetected and then striking quickly with deadly force.

Special operations forces use the most sophisticated and specialized weapons available, depending on the job at hand. The following are just some of the weapons and equipment available to special operations teams.

M4 Carbine

The 5.56mm **M4** rifle is compact at 30 inches (76 cm) and lightweight at just 5.65 pounds (2.56 kg). It features a silencer, night-vision scope, and targeting laser. It can also be equipped with a grenade launcher under the barrel.

MP-5

The **MP-5** is a 9mm submachine gun used in tight quarters, such as urban assault missions and raids.

Beretta 9mm Pistol

Lightweight and easy to hide, the **Beretta** is the general-use pistol of the U.S. military.

Ground Laser Target Designator

One of the most important jobs of special operations teams is to spot targets for strike aircraft. Soldiers a safe distance away on the ground do this by aiming a portable laser at the target. Incoming smart bombs sense the laser energy and guide themselves down toward the target with very high accuracy.

Night Vision Goggles

The latest night vision equipment is smaller and lighter than goggles of even just a few years ago. They also give special

ops soldiers clearer images, even in near total darkness. Night vision devices can be mounted to gun scopes, or work on a soldier's helmet. The devices magnify light from the moon or stars millions of times.

Where On The Web?

http://www.af.mil/
Official site of the U.S. Air Force. Excellent selection of photos, artwork, and diagrams, plus news stories.

http://www.army.mil/
Official site of the U.S. Army.

http://www.navy.mil/
Official site of the U.S. Navy.

http://www.usmc.mil/
Official site of the U.S. Marine Corps.

http://www.odci.gov/cia/publications/factbook/
Facts and figures of all the world's countries, compiled by the United States Central Intelligence Agency (CIA).

http://www.defenselink.mil/pubs/almanac/
Defense Almanac, a site filled with facts and statistics about the United States Department of Defense.

Glossary

Cold War

Shortly after World War II, the United States and the Soviet Union entered into a "cold war," which meant that the two countries were enemies to each other, but didn't actually get into a shooting war. Instead, the Cold War was waged diplomatically, and it was marked by a great buildup of weapons and troops. The Cold War ended as the Soviet Union broke up in the late 1980s and early 1990s.

early warning radar

Sophisticated radar that detects when enemy planes are entering friendly territory. In war, it is common practice to first destroy early warning radar sites so that the air force can then fly missions with a greater element of surprise.

reconnaissance

Finding the location of the enemy. "Recon" missions help commanders decide which forces to send into enemy territory.

smart bomb

A bomb or missile that navigates its way to a target, usually by following a laser beam "painted" on the target by a plane or special operations soldier on the ground. Smart bombs are usually very accurate.

supersonic

Faster than the speed of sound.

Index